THOROUGHBASS METHOD

Hermann Keller

THOROUGHBASS METHOD

WITH EXCERPTS FROM THE THEORETICAL WORKS
OF PRAETORIUS, NIEDT, TELEMANN, MATTHESON,
HEINICHEN, J. S. & C. P. E. BACH, QUANTZ, AND
PADRE MATTEI, AND NUMEROUS EXAMPLES FROM THE
LITERATURE OF THE 17TH AND 18TH CENTURIES

Translated and edited by CARL PARRISH

W · W · NORTON & COMPANY · INC · NEW YORK

Originally published in Germany as *Schule des Generalbassspiels* by Hermann Keller
© Bärenreiter-Verlag Karl Vötterle KG 1950.

Library of Congress Catalog Card No. 64–23882

Printed in the United States of America

2 3 4 5 6 7 8 9

Contents

Foreword

Anyone who assumes the task of publishing a method of thoroughbass playing today has no need of proving the necessity for it. There is no useful method except Riemann's small *Katechismus*, yet everyone who performs or arranges the music of the 17th and 18th centuries is forced to come to terms continually with the problems of thoroughbass. The reprinting of old sources (Praetorius, Telemann, C. P. E. Bach, Quantz), important though it is for the theoretical foundation of thoroughbass technique, cannot take the place of a practical thoroughbass method such as we need today. What is required is a work in which we can again learn, through *unrealized* and progressively arranged practice examples, what every musician knew then, namely how to improvise the realization of a figured bass at the instrument, without previous written preparation, and in doing so to adapt it each time to the particular circumstances.

No one will deny the need of achieving this objective, since there are still not many accompanists today who trust themselves (and whom a conductor will allow) to accompany a Bach cantata or Passion from the figures in the score. But this cannot be achieved by reprinting one of the great old thoroughbass methods, for these works are intolerably verbose as instruction books for students today, and, while thoroughbass is their main subject, they extend over every conceivable area of music. Others again, such as Mattheson's *Kleine Generalbass-Schule* or Telemann's *Singe- Spiel- und Generalbass-Übungen*, do not proceed beyond first principles.

Today it is customary for anyone who begins the study of thoroughbass playing to have acquired some previous knowledge of the simpler principles of harmony, or at least enough of the fundamental principles of music to suffice for the study of the present method. Accordingly, the first part, which treats of the meaning of the figures and of their use in four-part, note-against-note writing, can be more briefly treated than in the 18th-century methods. The crucial part of our book lies in the second part, the examples from 17th- and 18th-century compositions; that is, in the application of "school knowledge" to the multifarious and living music of the Baroque era. From the basic theoretical works of that period we have chosen only what the practical musician must know; the scholar will always have to refer to the sources themselves. The present method, though, within its limits may help to supply the practical musician with the foundations for a stylistically suitable performance of the music of the Baroque.

Much of importance is yet to be done in this area, for there is still a wide gap between knowledge and practice. In the last century we were given many editions that were unobjectionable from a scholarly standpoint but artistically unsatisfactory (I am thinking now, among other things, about many cadences of Chrysander in the oratorios of Handel, or Seiffert's editing of Handel's organ concertos). Or there were new editions that were musically of high quality but stylistically impossible (e.g. of violin concertos by outstanding violin virtuosos). For some years now it has seemed as though we have at last achieved the necessary synthesis—that is, acquiring the scholarly knowledge of the performance principles of the thorough-bass period as an obvious foundation, but then fostering beyond it that artistic freedom without which music cannot even exist (e.g. Arnold Schering, Friedrich Blume). It is hoped that the present method will provide the student with a skill—not only a knowledge—that may later qualify him for this freedom, insofar as his artistic powers permit.

It is plain to the writer that such a goal will be reached only in part through this first attempt at a modern thoroughbass method; certain unfortunate condensations and limitations were necessary, principally because of the lack of space enjoined by the cost of publication. In spite of that, publisher and author hope that the method may be assiduously used in institutions where church and school music are taught, in musicological proseminars, in conducting and composition classes of conservatories (where, with appropriate oral supplementation by the teacher, it could be used in teaching harmony, and would be more stimulating for students than most of the dry instruction of this subject), and above all by the many, even the amateurs, who are concerned with the execution or arranging of old music for church, home, or concert hall. It is with all these in mind that the method was planned. Since the examples have been taken from the best literature of the Baroque period, there is also the possibility that the method may well be used for practical music-making, and that would be pre-eminently in the spirit of the period.

The reader who has worked through this method will then seek to penetrate further into the material by himself, to read the sources himself, and to educate himself in the very rich literature that we have in the works of Bach and Handel, in the monuments of musical art of the 17th and 18th centuries, and other original editions. There is no end to learning! And finally, in whatever new ways a new harmony and a new harmony teaching may evolve, thoroughbass holds good as the foundation of the music of the 17th and 18th centuries and thereby of our own music also, and no one may be called "a solid musician" (in the words of F. E. Niedt) who does not master it thoroughly.

Hermann Keller

Stuttgart, Summer of 1931

Foreword to the Fourth Edition

In the more than 20 years since the first appearance of this method, many requests and suggestions for improving and supplementing it have been made to the author. The present version, enlarged and—in the opening part —substantially revised, attempts to take them into account. Just as in the 17th and 18th centuries almost all thoroughbass methods introduced the beginner at the same time into music theory in a practical manner, so it is hoped that this new version will enable the teacher to help the student go far enough in a short time without a harmony method so that the principles of harmony of the Vienna Classicists and of the 19th century may present few difficulties to him. But play, always play; don't write out exercises! The newly added final chapter offers suggestions for recapitulating the material learned and, to the accomplished thoroughbass player, for turning with artistic freedom and yet with stylistic faithfulness above and beyond the merely correct to the thoroughbass practice of the music of the 17th and 18th centuries, particularly in the music of the early Baroque and 18th-century opera. In this, however, only a few suggestions have sufficed; he who has gone thus far has no further need of a method.

Hermann Keller

Stuttgart, 1955

Hermann Keller's *Schule des Generalbassspiels*, which is presented here in English translation, is not unknown to American students of Baroque music. Since it first appeared in 1931 it has enjoyed a certain currency among harpsichord players in the United States—even those not able to read the German text—because of its representative and varied collection of musical examples from the 17th and 18th centuries. Through these practice examples alone it filled a need that is not met by any other book on the subject of thoroughbass, for Professor Keller selected them with care and perception from the varied repertory of sacred and secular music and the various styles of instrumental music of that period.

It seemed essential that an English translation be made, for the work is historically arranged from the beginning of the second section, and it includes many selections from writings about the realization of thoroughbass from Michael Praetorius to C. P. E. Bach, in addition to pertinent musical illustrations by these authors. Also, Keller himself has added valuable comments on the music and the varying kinds of realization that were expected of the accompanist according to the different epochs within the period, and the different styles of music for which an accompaniment is to be supplied.

His Method was published in a revised edition in 1959, in which the opening chapter on the fundamental principles of thoroughbass realization and of chord connection was considerably altered, and a wholly new chapter added at the end, which is a sort of summary treating of certain aspects of thoroughbass playing either not taken up or merely touched upon in the rest of the book. In other respects the two editions are the same except for the correction in the later volume of some minor details.

The translator wishes to acknowledge Professor Keller's kindness in clarifying a few passages from the authors whose writings on thoroughbass he has quoted, where the meaning seemed obscure.

C. P.

The Literature about Thoroughbass Playing

A. The Early Period (1600–50)

MAX SCHNEIDER: *Die Anfänge des Basso continuo und seiner Bezifferung* ("The Beginnings of Basso Continuo and its Figuring"), 1918 (contains, among other materials, 108 pages of musical examples from about 1600).

OTTO KINKELDEY: *Orgel und Klavier in der Musik des 16. Jahrhunderts* ("Organ and Harpsichord in the Music of the 16th Century"), 1910 (with 86 pages of musical examples from the second half of the 16th century).

MICHAEL PRAETORIUS: *Syntagma musicum, Tomus tertius* ("Treatise on Music, Book Three"), 1619; modern edition by Ed. Bernouli, 1916 (the basic source work for the music of the first half of the 17th century).

HEINRICH SCHÜTZ: Preface to the *Historia der frölichen und Siegreichen Aufferstehung* ("Story of the Joyous and Victorious Resurrection"), 1623; modern reprint in Bärenreiter Edition, 1927.

HEINRICH ALBERT: Preface to *Anderer Theil der Arien . . .* ("Another Part of the Arias . . ."), 1640; modern edition in *Denkmäler deutscher Tonkunst*, XII.

FRIEDRICH BLUME: *Zur Generalbasspraxis der Schütz-Zeit* ("On the Practice of Thoroughbass at the Time of Schütz"), *Musikantengilde*, 1927, no. 4.

B. The Period of the Domination of Thoroughbass (1650–1750)

The period of the great systematic thoroughbass methods. The most important among them are:

FRIDERICH ERHARD NIEDT: *Musici Musikalische Handleitung oder Gründlicher Unterricht, Vermittelst welchen ein Liebhaber der Edlen Music in kurtzer Zeit sich so weit perfectioniren kan, dass Er nicht allein den General-Bass nach denen gesetzten deutlichen und wenigen Regeln fertig spielen sondern auch folglich allerley Sachen selbst componiren und ein rechtschaffener Organist und Musicus heissen könne.* ("The Musician's Vademecum, or fundamental instructions by which a lover of noble music can perfect himself so far in a short time that he may not only play thoroughbass according to its few and clearly ordered rules, but then compose also various kinds of pieces himself, and may be called a solid organist and musician".), Hamburg, 1700. This work, of which only a few copies have survived, is of particular interest to us because J. S. Bach based the first chapter of his own thoroughbass method on it (see below); it is an excellent method, both stylistically and in substance.

JOHANN DAVID HEINICHEN: *Der Generalbass in der Composition* ("Thoroughbass in Composition"), Dresden, 1728. Gives complete instruction in composition, in 960 pages. Mattheson wrote: ". . . it rightly deserves to stand at the top, and it would only be superfluous here to enlarge upon the praise given this work, since it must already be in the hands of everyone."

JOHANN MATTHESON: *Kleine Generalbass-Schule* ("Little Method of Thoroughbass"), Hamburg, 1735. Treats of the elementary principles of music and of thoroughbass.

JOHANN MATTHESON: *Grosse Generalbass-Schule, oder: der exemplarischen Organisten-Probe zweite verbesserte und vermehrte Auflage* ("Grand Method of Thoroughbass, or second corrected and enlarged edition of Specimen Examinations for Organists"), Hamburg, 1731. Contains twice 24 extended figured basses, with instructions for their realization. An important work, too little known and used today.

C. From the Late Period (Middle to End of the 18th Century)

CARL PHILIPP EMANUEL BACH: *Versuch über die wahre Art, das Clavier zu spielen*[1] ("Essay on the True Manner of playing Keyboard Instruments"), Berlin,

[1] English translation, *Essay on the True Art of Playing Keyboard Instruments*, by William Mitchell, New York, 1949. [Ed.]

 1753 and later; modern edition by W. Niemann, 1906 (unfortunately with omission of the part that lays the foundation for the actual thoroughbass instruction).

JOHANN JOACHIM QUANTZ: *Versuch einer Anweisung, die Flöte traversiere zu spielen; mit verschiedenen, zur Beförderung des guten Geschmacks in der praktischen Musik dienlichen Anmerkungen* ("Essay on Instruction in Playing the Transverse Flute; with various useful remarks about the promoting of good taste in practical music"), 1752; modern edition by A. Schering, 1906. This famous work and the equally celebrated treatise by C. P. E. Bach complement each other: Bach writes from the standpoint of the accompanist, Quantz from that of the soloist. Coming at the end of the Baroque period, each makes extraordinary demands for refinement of execution, and shows ornamentation at its highest level of development.

In Italy, Padre Stanislao Mattei (1750–1825), pupil of Padre Martini and teacher of Rossini and Donizetti, in his *Practica d'accompagnamento sopra bassi numerati* ("The Practice of Accompaniment on Figured Basses"), assembled valuable examples for exercise, and with it the classical Italian school (Durante, Fenaroli, and others) came to an end. Some of his examples are included in the present method. Also, certain keyboard methods of the 18th century and later contain instructions in thoroughbass playing, such as those of Marpurg (1755), Löhlein (1765), Türk (1789), A. E. Müller (1804), and others.

In the 19th century, the art of thoroughbass playing was lost, although the figuring of basses continued to be used in most harmony instruction books. Only since Hugo Riemann's *Katechismus des Generalbassspiels* ("Catechism of Thoroughbass Playing"), first edition, 1899, did a revival of playing from figured basses occur, hesitantly at first, but more generally practiced today.

F. T. Arnold's valuable work, *The Art of Accompaniment from a Thorough-bass* (London, 1931, 918 pp.), gives a comprehensive presentation of the whole period, with excerpts from the authors mentioned here and also from the works of L. Viadana (1602), A. Agazzari (the source for Praetorius; 1607), A. Banchieri (1611), J. Staden (1626), G. Sabbatini (1628), W. Ebner (1631), L. Penna (1672), M. Locke (1673), St. Lambert (1680), A. Werckmeister (1698), F. Gasparini (1708), C. Schröter (1772), and still others.

Georg Philipp Telemann: *Singe-, Spiel- und Generalbass-Übungen* ("Thoroughbass Exercises, Vocal and Instrumental"), Hamburg, 1733–34; modern edition by M. Seiffert, 1921. Contains 48 vocal pieces with the basses realized.

Johann Sebastian Bach: *Vorchriften und Grundsätze zum vierstimmigen spielen des Generalbasses oder Accompagnement für seine Scholaren in der Musik* ("Precepts and Principles for Four-part Playing of Thoroughbass, or Accompaniment, for his Music Students"), 1738. Printed in Spitta, II, 913ff. [Eng. transl. III, Appendix XII, 315ff.] Chapters one through seven are an abridgement of the method of F. E. Niedt (see above). [For a description and discussion of this work, as well as of the short list of rules of thoroughbass that Bach compiled for his wife Anna Magdalena, see Spitta, *J. S. Bach*, III, 347–48, Eng. transl. Ed.]

Mention should also be made of the thoroughbass methods of: Fabricius (1675), A. Werckmeister (1698), Böddecker (1701), and "An Anonymous One" (1689 and later); French methods by Boyvin (1700) and Dandrieu (c. 1725) ought also to be cited.

What is Thoroughbass?

Nothing other than bass notes with figures that indicate full-voiced harmony, and according to whose indications full chords are played on the harpsichord (or some other keyboard instrument) . . .

Mattheson

No one who understands music will deny that basso continuo, or thorough-bass, as it is called, is one of the most important and fundamental parts of musical knowledge, next to composition. For whence does it arise other than from composition itself? And what else does thoroughbass playing mean than to invent extemporaneously, or to compose to a single given bass part the other parts in full harmony?

Heinichen

Thoroughbass is the absolute foundation of music and it is played with both hands in such a way that the left hand takes the written notes, while the right hand plays notes consonant and dissonant to them, so that this may give a pleasing harmony to the glory of God and the licit delight of the spirit. The end and aim of thoroughbass, like that of all music, should be only the glory of God and the refreshment of the spirit. Where this is not kept in mind there is no real music, but only a devilish kind of bawling and singsong.

J. S. Bach, after *F. E. Niedt*

PART I

The Foundations of Thoroughbass Playing

CHAPTER 1
Summary of Chord Principles

Concerning the elements of music, "not much will be said here, for it is presupposed that whoever wishes to learn thoroughbass not only knows the notes but understands the intervals according to their distances—either through previous practice or some other foretaste of music—and must know the different time values."[1]

As the first exercise, the student should play triads in all keys in four voices, in close position of the three upper voices, and in the octave-, fifth-, and third-positions. E.g.:

1.

The 8ve-position in G maj.   The 3rd-position in G♯ min.   The 5th-position in E♭ maj.

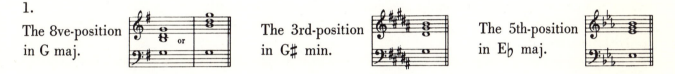

In thoroughbass figuring, a triad is required wherever there is no sign. If the third of the triad is changed, a ♯, ♮, or ♭ appears under the bass note.[2] E.g.:

2.

In G min.   in F min.   in B♭ maj.

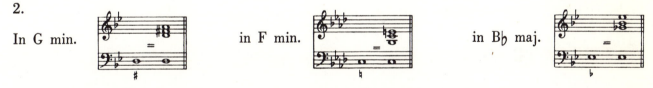

EXERCISE: Connect the triad on the first degree of the scale (the tonic) with that of the fifth degree (the dominant). In doing this, the bass goes from root to root, and the other voices proceed in the most direct way, keeping the common tones between successive triads in the same voice:

3.

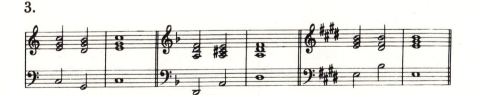

---

[1] This is a quotation from J. S. Bach's method of thoroughbass, Chapter IV (see Spitta, *J. S. Bach*, Eng. transl., III, 319). [Ed.]

[2] Although the older thoroughbass methods require that the figures be put above the notes, here, following the general present usage, they are put under the notes. [H. K.]

Play these progressions in all keys and in all three positions.

EXERCISE: Connect the triad on the first degree with that on the fourth degree (the subdominant).

4.

Play this progression also in all keys and in the three positions.

EXERCISE: Connect the triads of the first, fourth, and fifth degrees, one after another (the perfect cadence). In so doing, one voice must not form an octave or a perfect fifth with another (forbidden parallel octaves and fifths).

5. Therefore, not

6. but (through contrary motion).

Play these progressions in all keys and positions.

  Other exercises in chord connection:

7.   8.   9.

Play these examples in all keys.

The Inversion of Triads

In the first inversion of a chord, the third lies in the bass. This chord, in thoroughbass figuring, is numbered as the "six-three chord," after the distance of the next tone of the triad from the bass, or, according to the abbreviated form generally used, the "sixth chord":

In four-part setting, either the tonic or the fifth of the triad is usually doubled, but not the third:

10.

If, however, the sixth is raised as the leading tone, it is not doubled:

11.

A common abbreviation for the raised sixth is 6̸, rather than 6♯.

The second inversion, in which the fifth is in the bass, is called the "six-four chord" (G to C is a fourth, G to E a sixth; the third—from C to E—is not considered):

The most frequent use of this chord is as a chord of suspension to the dominant (6 goes to 5, 4 goes to 3):

12.

Play this succession in all keys.

The knowledge gained up to this point is already sufficient for chorale playing; Nos. 47 through 50 (pp. 18–19) may even now be performed.

Seventh Chords

Seventh chords originated from triads in which the octave of one chord descends in passing to the next chord. For that reason the seventh is always taken downward. Such progressions are indicated by figures placed one after another:

13.   14.

The seventh chord on the fifth degree (the dominant seventh chord) frequently takes the place of the simple dominant. The figure employed is 7 (abbreviated from $\begin{smallmatrix}7\\5\\3\end{smallmatrix}$).

15.   16.

Play these examples in all keys.

The Inversions of Seventh Chords

The first inversion, with the third in the bass, is called the "six-five-three" chord, or, more simply, the "six-five" chord:

The second inversion, with the fifth in the bass, is called the "six-four-three" chord, or, more simply, the "four-three" chord:

The third inversion, with the seventh in the bass, is called the "six-four-two" chord, or, more simply, the "two" chord:

Since the seventh degree descends stepwise, the two chord resolves to the chord of the sixth:

Examples of progressions employing the three inversions of the seventh chord:

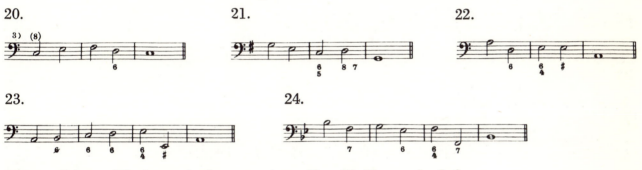

Play these examples in all keys.

Exercises with Triads, Seventh Chords, and Their Inversions

Play in all keys. (The basses in these exercises—Nos. 26–30—are by J. S. Bach.)[4]

25.

26.

---

[3] The sign (8) means "begin in the octave-position." [H. K.]

[4] The examples to which Keller refers are more or less modified versions of certain examples in J. S. Bach's *Rules . . . for Playing Thoroughbass,* which is printed as Appendix XII of Spitta's *J. S. Bach* (Eng. transl., III, 315–47). No. 26 in Keller is taken from no. 4 in Bach, no. 27 from no. 6, no. 28 from no. 7, no. 29 from no. 13, and no. 30 from no. 14. Only the first part of each example (about a third or less of the whole) is given. [Ed.]

27.

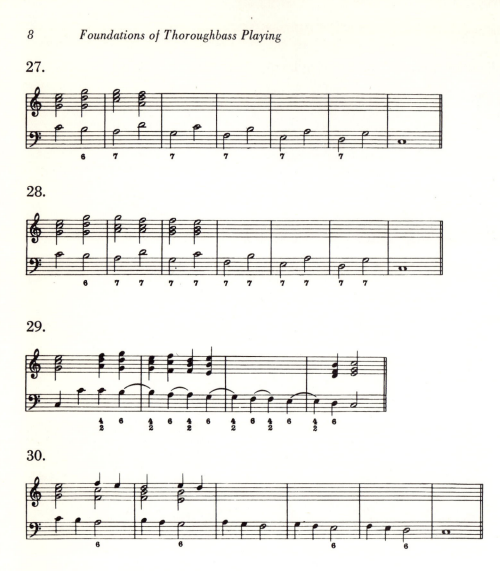

28.

29.

30.

Non-Harmonic Tones

Quickly moving tones that are foreign to the underlying harmony—passing tones and changing tones—are not harmonized:

31.

Anticipations and suspensions are indicated by adjacent numbers:

32.

The Suspension

This is a dissonance occurring on an accented part of the measure. The suspension tone should, as far as possible, be in the same voice in the preceding harmony, thus:

33.

not

The most frequent suspensions are: 4 to 3, 9 to 8, and 7 to 6.

34.

Exercises with non-harmonic tones:

35.

36.

37.

38.

39.

Padre Mattei: 1. Modulations over Figured Basses, from C Major to All Major and Minor Keys

40.

To major keys:

to G major

to D major

to A major

to E major

to B major

to F♯ major

to D♭ major

to A♭ major

to E♭ major

to B♭ major

to F major

To minor keys:

to A minor

to E minor

to B minor

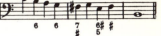

to F♯ minor

to C♯ minor

to A♭ minor

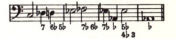

to E♭ minor

to B♭ minor

to F minor

to C minor

to G minor

to D minor

These modulations may also be used to great advantage as exercises in memory training and transposition by playing each one, first from the notes, then repeating it from memory, and then transposing it from memory to other keys. Take care especially that the upper voices move stepwise as much as possible.

Padre Mattei: 2. Four Longer Figured Basses

41.

42.

43.

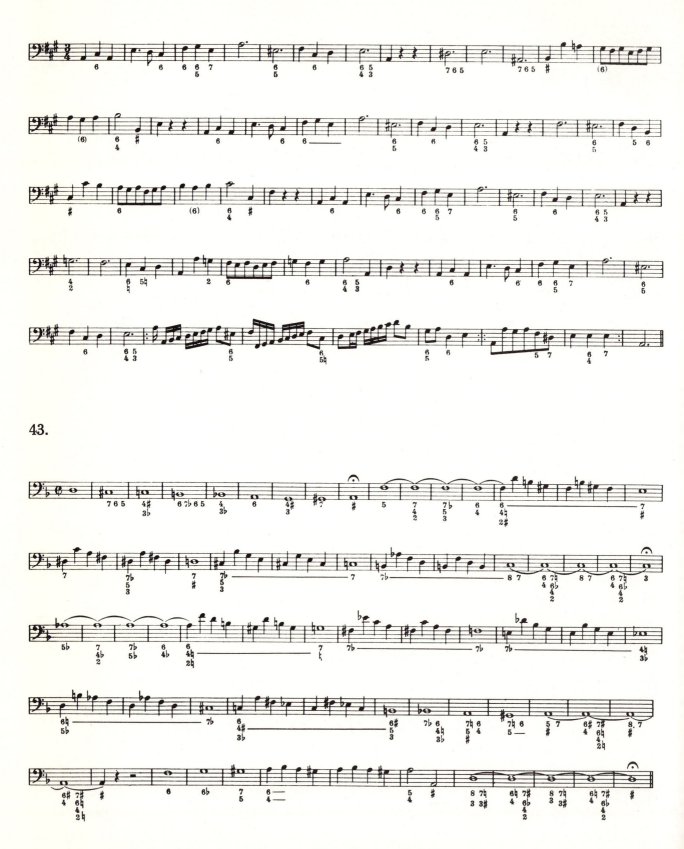

44.

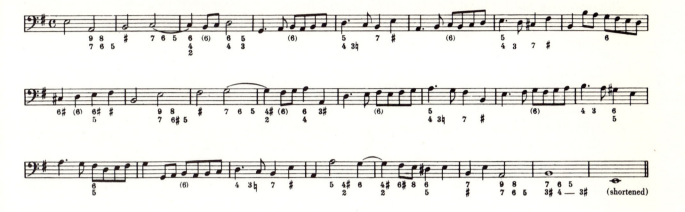

These four exercises may be regarded as preliminary studies for those of Mattheson (see Nos. 75–79). After they are solved harmonically, one should try to treat them as the basses of definite, though imagined, compositions: the first and fourth, for example, as slow movements of a trio sonata; the second as a minuet in rondo form; the fourth I imagine as the Dies irae of a Requiem.

Summary of Figures Used in Thoroughbass

The figures indicate the intervals to be played above the given bass, either at their actual distances or in a higher octave-transposition. The usual abbreviations are as follows:

1. The absence of a figure indicates that the triad is to be played.
2. A ♯, ♮, or ♭ by itself applies to the third.
3. An oblique line through a number (mostly through 4 and 5) or—for reasons of clarity—next to a figure, means a semitone raising of the interval so marked.
4. The following are always abbreviated:

$$6 \text{ for } \begin{smallmatrix}6\\3\end{smallmatrix} \quad 7 \text{ for } \begin{smallmatrix}7\\5\\3\end{smallmatrix} \quad \begin{smallmatrix}6\\5\end{smallmatrix} \text{ for } \begin{smallmatrix}6\\5\\3\end{smallmatrix} \quad \begin{smallmatrix}4\\3\end{smallmatrix} \text{ for } \begin{smallmatrix}6\\4\\3\end{smallmatrix}$$

$$2, \text{ or } \begin{smallmatrix}4\\2\end{smallmatrix} \text{ for } \begin{smallmatrix}6\\4\\2\end{smallmatrix} \quad (\text{sometimes also for } \begin{smallmatrix}5\\2\end{smallmatrix})$$

5. Figures occurring one above the other are played simultaneously; those occurring one after another are played consecutively (voice-leading).

6. A horizontal line means that the figures continue (i.e. there is no change of harmony on the following notes).

7. Short oblique dashes mean that the figuring is repeated.

8. "Tasto solo" or "t. s." or "o" means that only the bass is played (this occurs especially in pedal points).

9. Figures beneath a rest indicate the prevailing harmony.

10. Passing tones and changing tones in the bass, especially those in smaller note values, receive no figuring and are not harmonized.

In the early thoroughbass period, a ♭ stands generally for a lowering of pitch, a ♯ for a raising (instead of ♮; see, e.g. No. 66, m. 12). The diminished fifth was also indicated at that time with a ♭, if it was proper to the scale.

CHAPTER 2

Thoroughbass Playing in Simple Four-Part Style, Note-Against-Note

The rules given up to this point do not extend far enough to guide the player through all the difficulties encountered in playing a basso continuo, but "the remaining precautions that one must keep in mind are shown better through oral than written instructions," and they reveal themselves mostly in actual practice.[1] The strict four-part style, which will be taken up now, formed the basis of continuo playing in Bach's time, when the realization was not always in that one style, as it customarily is today, unfortunately. In order to accompany well in two, three, or many parts, one must first of all be able to play correctly in four parts, and this section serves to that end. The left hand plays only the given bass, the right hand the realization in close position, in a register never higher than that of the solo voice.[2]

At the outset, two pieces may be cited from Telemann's *Sing-, Spiel- und Generalbassübungen* that are realized by the composer himself, and which show that the uppermost part of the basso continuo can at times go along in unison with the melody voice, or it can be made more independent. Even parallel octaves in an accompanying part are unobjectionable, especially if the principal part such as a violin, for example, moves now in a high range, now in a low one. (One need only think of one of the Telemann songs as sung by a male rather than a female voice; all the unisons then become parallel octaves. I mention this because there is a purist view—e.g. that of Johannes Schreyer—that would forbid and exclude parallel octaves with the leading voice.)

---

[1] The quotation is the last sentence of the short rules of thoroughbass that Bach noted down for Anna Magdalena's *Clavierbuch* of 1725 (see Spitta, *J. S. Bach*, Eng. transl., III, 348). [Ed.]

[2] The last phrase of this sentence appears to be contradicted by the very first examples that Keller presents after this (Nos. 45 and 46). In answer to a question about this, Dr. Keller says that his statement is to be regarded only as a rule of thumb, and that any departure from it made on musical grounds would be unobjectionable. [Ed.]

45. *Seltenes Glück* ("Rare Fortune")

Ein stand, der ohn ge-fahr ist, ein gu-ter ruhm, der wahr ist, ein ca-pi-tal, das baar___ ist, ein

es - sen, das fein gahr ist, ein trunck, der frisch und klar ist, ein weib, das gu - ter haar ist und

un - ter zwan-zig jahr ist: wenn diß zu - sam-men dar___ ist, das heist ein glück, das rar ist.

A place that is without danger,
A good reputation that is deserved,
Money that is ready at hand,
Food that is well cooked,
Drink that is cool and clear,
A woman who keeps house well
And who is under twenty;
If all these are there together,
That's what is called rare good fortune.

From Telemann's remarks to measures 11–14: "Here, and at several places, the upper dissonant figures are taken as passing tones, and emphasis is put on the second note." [In reply to a question concerning Telemann's remark, Dr. Keller explains this passage, which, as he says, is not clearly expressed, as follows: "The first and third quarter notes in measures 11 through 14 ought not be treated as suspensions that would be figured as 9-8, 6-5, or 4-3, but rather as accented passing tones, in which the figuring is based only on the harmonies of the second and fourth beats of the measure." Ed.]

[3] In the 18th century, especially in Handel and Telemann, the figure 6 by itself sometimes stands for $\frac{6}{4}$. [H. K.]

46. *Die dürstige Natur* ("Thirsty Nature")

The earth itself drinks rain and snow,
And trees must feed on sap,
The sea drinks from the air, the sun from the sea,
The moon must draw on the sun for its strength.
Friends, you know this;
Why, then, do you grumble if meanwhile
I, too, take a little drink.

The minuets by Telemann that for pedagogical reasons appear later on (Nos. 107–09) may be played here, in view of their technical simplicity.

⁴ Or:

"In loud music it is good" to repeat the chords on each eighth note, "but not in soft music and certainly not on organs, where . . . the notes are connected" (Telemann).

As the first independent exercises in playing a basso continuo with a given upper voice, certain chorale settings from the 17th and 18th centuries follow. These can be played in different ways: first on the harpsichord or piano in close position (the right hand taking three parts, the left hand taking the bass), or on the organ (the right hand taking three parts, the pedals taking the bass). Later, one should try playing the settings on the harpsichord or piano in open position, and on the organ with two manuals and pedal (bringing out the cantus firmus). Always *play* the exercises; never write them out!

47. From the Nuremberg Songbook, 1677

My own dear Jesus, what is Thy offence
That such harsh judgement is pronounced upon Thee?
What is Thy guilt? Into what crimes hast Thou fallen?

48. From the Darmstadt Songbook, 1699

Let us praise the Lord, O ye Christians everywhere,
Come, let us render thanks to our God with sweet sounds.
He is freed from the bonds of death,
[Our] Samson, who came down from Heaven,
Descended from the Lion of Judah,
Christ Jesus hath arisen, the bitter fight is over;
Rejoice, ye Christians!

49. From the Nuremberg Songbook, 1677

Arouse thyself, my feeble spirit,
And fulfill thy great desire
To receive with joy a little Child
Who is also called the Father.
This is the night in which He came
And took on human form,
Thereby to wed the world as His faithful bride.

50. From the Nuremberg Songbook, 1677

Happily will my heart leap up
As all the angels sing now for joy.
It hears, it hears how all the air
Doth loudly ring with full-voiced choir:
"Christ is born."

51. From Freylinghausen's Songbook, Halle, 1713

Up, Zion, up! Up, daughter, do not linger,
Thy King comes, graciously to embrace thee;
He burns with love, with compassion, and pity;
Hold thyself ready, that thy light dim not.
Let the lamps of thy faith always burn,
Let not thine eyes close now in sleep.

The following compositions by J. S. Bach (ten sacred songs with figured bass—Nos. 52 through 60 are from Schemelli's *Gesangbuch*, 1736; No. 61 is from Anna Magdalena Bach's *Notenbuch*, 1725) have often been realized for practical use. In published editions of them, two different tendencies may be distinguished: in one they are regarded as chorales, and for that reason the upper voice of the accompaniment throughout is in unison with the vocal part (Robert Franz, Ernst Naumann, and others); in the other they are treated as sacred songs, and the upper voice of the accompaniment is made independent of the vocal part (Hermann Roth). In general, the best procedure might be to retain the vocal line as the upper part [i.e. treat it as a chorale] except at those places where one might wish not to have the accompaniment duplicate certain Baroque embellishments in the vocal part. Occasionally (e.g. in No. 52, m. 11), the accompaniment can even be five-voiced if the figuring requires it.

52. *O Jesulein süss*

O sweet little Jesus, O gentle little Jesus,
Thou hast fulfilled Thy Father's will,
Thou hast come down from Thy heavenly kingdom
To become like us poor sinners,
O sweet little Jesus, O gentle little Jesus.

53. *Ihr Gestirn, ihr hohen Lüfte*

Ye stars, ye lofty winds, and thou, bright firmament,
Thou deep void, ye dark gulfs, that echo rends,
Exult with joy, let your song press through the clouds.

54. *Gieb dich zufrieden und sei stille*

Content thyself, and be at rest
In the God of thy love.
In Him rests the fullness of all joy;
Without Him thy cares are in vain.
He is thy well-spring and thy sun
That brightly shines each day
For thy happiness. Content thyself.

55. *Mein Jesu, was für Seelenweh*

My Jesus, what woe besets Thy soul
In Gethsemane, wherein Thou hast gone;
The anguish of death, the torment of hell,
And all Belial's brooks do hold Thee fast.
Thou dost quail, moan, tremble, and shudder,
And in distress dost raise Thy hands to heaven.

56. *So gehst du nun, mein Jesu, hin*

So goest Thou now, my Jesus
To suffer death for me,
For me, who am a sinner,
Who turns Thy joy to sadness.
Now go Thou on, Thou noble treasure,
And from my eyes shall flow
A sea of tears, with anguished cries,
To pour upon Thy suffering.

57. *Kommt wieder aus der finstern Gruft*

Come forth again from the dark tomb,
Ye souls devoted to God;
Take new courage, draw in fresh air,
Look up to Zion's heights;
For Jesus, who lay in the grave,
On the third day overcame the kingdom
Of death like a conquering hero.

58. *Jesus, unser Trost und Leben*

Jesus, our solace and our life,
Who was given over to death,
Did wondrously and mightily
Bring back life and victory.
He arose from the bonds of death
Like a victorious Prince.
Allelujah! Allelujah!

59. *Dir, dir Jehovah, will ich singen*

To Thee, to Thee, Jehovah, shall I sing,
For where, indeed, is such a God as Thou?
To Thee shall I bring my songs.
Give me the power of Thy spirit for that purpose,
That I may do it in the name of Jesus Christ,
So that through Him it may please Thee.

60. *So wünsch' ich mir zu guter lezt*

I would that at my end I might die in a blessed hour,
One that may bring joy for all my sorrows
And crown me with the heritage of heaven.
Come, gentle death, and show me where
My Friend doth graze in peace,
So that my soul, too, may desire
To turn from this world to Him.

61. *Bist du bei mir*

(not figured)

If thou be with me, I shall go with joy
To my death and to my peace . . .
Ah, how happy would be my end
If thy lovely hands would close my faithful eyes . . .

PART II

Thoroughbass Playing in the Practice of the 17th and 18th Centuries

CHAPTER 3
The Early Period (Until c. 1650)

As an introduction to this section, certain significant passages from Praetorius's *Syntagma Musicum*, Book III, may be quoted.

From Chapter 6 (Introduction): "How thoroughbass, *basso continuo*, or *basso pro organo* is to be understood; also, how the same is to be played and used; then, what is more important to recall in this connection, namely what is expected in general from the organist, lutenist, or harpist, and how each of these should play and use his instrument, according to its kind and character:

"What an organist should have as his distinctive qualities:

1. He must understand counterpoint or, at the very least, be able to sing perfectly . . .
2. He must thoroughly understand music written in score notation or in tablature . . .
3. He must also have a good ear and a fine sense of hearing . . ."

To illustrate the use of the figures, Praetorius gives the following example:

62.

"This is now notated with the signs and numbers above the thoroughbass thus:"

From Section 2 (Chapter 6): "How an organist should play any song or concerto is explained in the eight items that follow:

"1. . . . When the singer makes his diminutions and passages, let the accompanist proceed very simply from one note to the other. But then, when the singer, after performing many different *Movimenten*, beautiful *Diminutionen*, *Groppen*, *Tremoletten*, and *Trillen*,[1] must

---

[1] Of the untranslated terms in this paragraph, Praetorius defines *Diminutionen* as "coloraturas" (*Syntagma Musicum*, p. 232). The word *Movimenten* appears to be generally synonymous with it, having the same meaning as our "divisions" and "diminutions." The other terms—*Tremoletten*, *Groppen*, and *Trillen*—are various types of trills, illustrated by examples on pp. 235–37 of the *Syntagma*. [Ed.]

begin to sing the next notes plainly and simply because of shortness of breath, the organist should come in with beautiful *Diminutionen,* etc., playing these only with his right hand, and taking care to imitate what the singer had previously done in his *Movimenten,* diminutions, variations, etc., and therefore make them like an echo, as it were, until the singer recovers himself and can again let the charm of his art be heard and appreciated . . .

"2. . . . It is necessary, especially for someone who is inexperienced, to read through carefully and well beforehand the song that he will be accompanying . . . [This holds true even today!]

"3. . . . If a bass sings, the organist must make the cadences also in the bass; if a tenor, he must make them in the tenor, and so on[2] . . . although some may be of a different opinion about this matter.

"4. If a piece appears to be a fugue or a chorale, the organist should also . . . begin with only one part; but then when other voices are added to it he is free to play more voices as he sees fit. [See No. 106, m. 7.]

"5. When . . . all parts occur together, which is called by the Italians *ripieni concerti,* one should play the manuals and pedals on the organ with both hands and feet, but not add to it any further stops, for the milder and softer tone of the singers would then be overwhelmed by the loud sound of the many registers drawn in the organ; the latter would thus be so loud that the individual singers could not be heard. However, some . . . may be of the opinion that more stops should be pulled when the *ripieni concerti* or *pleni concentus* begins. It is still better if there are two manuals, for then one has a very soft organ in the one and something stronger in the other . . . [Even today the organ is frequently thickened in an unpleasant manner by the use of the full sound.]

"6. In realizing a figured bass, it is not necessary for the organist to be concerned about two fifths or two octaves, but rather about the register of the vocal part. Therefore, when a concerto is arranged *ad aequales,* or when a tenor or bass voice sings, the organist should never go above into the discant range, but remain in the lower range. On the other hand, when high discant voices sing, he should not stay in the lower range but remain in the higher one, although in the cadences he may indeed use the lower octave, for the melody is made more beautiful and graceful in that way.

"7. . . . the bass moves in four ways:

a. If it ascends by conjunct degrees, the right hand should descend in opposite motion, either conjunctly or by skips.

[2] Meaning that the cadence formula used in the voice should be doubled in that same voice part in the accompaniment. (See F. T. Arnold, *The Art of Accompaniment* . . . , p. 11ff.) [Ed.]

b. On the other hand, if the lower hand skips . . . one should proceed with the upper hand by steps, for it is not good to have skips in both hands at the same time, or to drop down, since it not only sounds gruff, unpleasant, and rude, but looks that way also . . .

c. If the bass climbs upwards with a *tirata*[3] and short running passages, one after another, the upper hand must remain in its place.

d. If there are disjunct quarter notes, each note must be accompanied with its own suitable harmony in the upper hand, as seen in the following example [in which four different cases—a) through d)—are illustrated]:

63.

Further on, Praetorius gives the following example, "for the sake of better explanation and understanding."

Bassus generalis:

64.

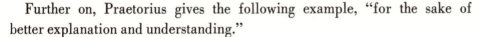

Resolutio:

65.

(This example shows clearly enough, in mm. 5 and 9, how lightly correct voice-leading was taken in continuo playing in the early part of the 17th century. See rule 6.)

---

[3] A Baroque ornament consisting of a scale passage that filled a large interval in a melody. [Ed.]

"N.B. This is to be noted particularly, also: If two or three voices are sung with the thoroughbass part from which the organist or lutenist plays, it is very good, almost necessary, even, to have the same thoroughbass part played by a bass instrument such as a bassoon, dolcian [another double-reed instrument], or trombone, or else—best of all—a bass viol . . . One can also have the thoroughbass part sung, for which purpose I should then apply the text underneath, as well as it will go." (Johann Hermann Schein expresses himself similarly in the Preface to his *Waldliederlein,* or *Musica boscareccia,* 1621.)

In the next section, Praetorius discusses "lutenists, harpists, etc., and how all that is played from a thoroughbass arranged for the organ may also be used by taking into consideration the lute, harp, theorbo, and similar instruments, and arranging it more suitably."

". . . They [the accompanying instruments] should always proceed with a steady, euphonious, and continuous harmony, so as to support the human voices, and sometimes play quietly and peacefully, sometimes loudly and vigorously, according to the character and number of voices; also according to the circumstances of the place and of the concerted group . . ." (The realization of the *basso continuo* on the lute is not treated in the present method, since it is principally governed by the technique of lute playing.)

Thus great importance is given in this period to the kind of sound produced and to improvisatory performance, much less to voice-leading in the *basso continuo.* As great as the freedom was in choice of thoroughbass instrument and in volume and manner of setting, so great was the responsibility that this kind of music placed upon the executants. In general, we are still rather confused today in regard to the early Baroque technique of improvisatory embellishment, and none of the editions with which I am acquainted has dared up to now to apply the directions of Praetorius, quoted above, in actual practice. Above all, there is still a lack of singers at the present time who study to revive this tradition; if there were more of them, accompanists who are knowledgeable in it would be found more readily.

Thus if the music of Schütz is sung without embellishment, it should be accompanied also without embellishment, in simple, chordal style, but appropriately in regard to the range and number of parts in relation to the principal voices. Therefore, in the following example from Schütz, the accompaniment must be different if it is sung by two sopranos rather than by two tenors; different also if the principal voice parts are sung by soloists rather than by a small choir.[4]

From the Preface by Heinrich Schütz to the *Historia von der frölichen und siegreichen Aufferstehung* . . . : "The Evangelist can be sung to a positive organ, or else to a harpsichord, lute, pandora, etc., as one pleases, since

---

[4] Schering (*op. cit.,* p. 149) advises accompanying pieces from the time of Schütz that are for a few voices, or even for solo voices, in only three parts, as was customary in the 17th century (according to a statement by Heinichen). [H. K.]

the words of the Evangelist have been put under the *basso continuo* right up to the end. But if it is the organist who will represent this part, he should keep in mind that as long as the recitative is on a single [repeated] note he should continually make appropriate embellishing runs or passages under [the vocal part] on the organ or harpsichord with his hand, which will give the right style to the work. And he should do this in all the other recitative passages; otherwise they do not have their proper effect."

From the Preface by Heinrich Albert to the First and Second Parts of the *Arias*: ". . . One thing you must have foremost in mind: you should know how to treat the thoroughbass according to the possibilities of the instrument, and you should not fall upon every note [of the thoroughbass] with great handfuls, and chop away at them as you would at cabbage . . .

". . . Note that you should always hold such harmonies closely, one after another, and take great care to have an elegant progression of these in such a way that for the most part the third is nearest the bass when the latter is high, but the fifth when it is low."[5] [Albert's other rules obviously follow those of Praetorius.]

66. Heinrich Schütz: *Kleines geistliches Konzert* No. 14.

[5] What Albert means by this sentence is that the parts should proceed as much as possible in contrary motion. In the sentence that follows (not quoted by Keller), he goes on to state that by doing so consecutive fifths and octaves may be avoided. See Arnold, *op. cit.*, p. 126ff. [Ed.]

O help us, Christ, Thou Son of God, by Thy bitter sorrows,
To be ever subject to Thee, to avoid all evil,
To ponder, for our benefit, upon Thy death and the reason therefor,
To render our thank-offering to Thee, even though we are poor and weak.

67. Heinrich Albert: *Herbstlied* ("Autumn Song")

Simon Dach

Forest and field now rise again to lament,
For the fierce cold will banish all pleasure.
The north wind howls, whistles, and calls
Here and there, in the air;
All the leaves fall because of the harsh weather he brings.

68. Heinrich Albert: *Vorjahrslied* ("Spring Song")

Simon Dach

We see now the whole house of the earth rejoice,
The lovely joy of May entices village and town outdoors.
My heart begins to wander when the creatures of the air do soar
And make a song ring out so that hill and valley resound.

69. Adam Krieger: *Abendlied* ("Evening Song")

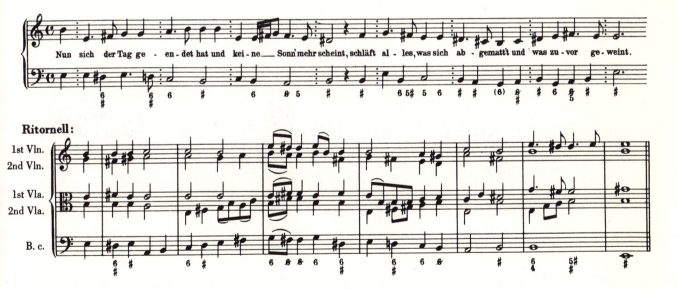

Now the day has ended, and the sun shines no more;
Everyone who had wept before and was wearied sleeps now.

CHAPTER 4
Thoroughbass in the Second Half of the 17th Century

The development of music (and of thoroughbass simultaneously with it) in the second half of the 17th century is connected with the rise of the violin and of chamber music in Italy. The most significant works of this epoch are the chamber compositions of Arcangelo Corelli (1653–1713):

24 Sonate da Chiesa a tre: Due Violini, e Violone o Arcileuto, col Basso per l'Organo, Opp. I (1681) and III (1689);

24 Sonate da Camera a tre: Due Violini, e Violone o Cembalo, Opp. II (1685) and IV (1694);

6 Sonate a Violino e Violone o Cimbalo, Op. V (1700);

Concerti grossi con duoi Violini, e Violoncello di Concertino obligati, e duoi altri Violini, Viola e Basso di Concerto Grosso ad arbitrio che si potranno radoppiare, Op. VI (1714).

As an example of the ornamenting technique of that time, a movement from the first Violin Sonata by Corelli follows, with the composer's own embellishments:

70.

[to be continued
by the student]

In both trio-sonata movements by Buxtehude that follow, the viola da gamba (which can be replaced here by the viola or cello) proceeds at times with the bass, but at other times as an independent middle voice. Here, as in the two trio-sonata movements of Corelli, only seldom does an interval occur in the figures (such as a suspension) that is not contained in the principal voices. The accompaniment, therefore, should be as simple as possible, and should merely follow the lines of the leading voices in broad outlines. The participation of the accompaniment in a solo sonata is naturally more independent, but even there it should not aim at attaining the significance of a second obbligato part. All early teachings of thoroughbass emphasize time and again that "the thoroughbass is not to be conceived of as something with which one concertizes, but only with which to accompany concertizing parts" (Heinichen). The notes in small print (in No. 73) indicate editorial suggestions. Compare also the practical editions of Corelli's Sonatas.

Two Trio Sonata Movements by Dietrich Buxtehude

71. From the third of the seven *Sonate a due, Violino e Viola da gamba,*
Opera prima (1686)

72. From the fourth of the seven *Sonate a due, Violino e Viola da gamba*
con Cembalo (1686)

Two Trio Sonata Movements by Arcangelo Corelli

73. From the third *Sonata da chiesa*, Op. 3

The difficulties of the following example lie in the running basses—whose passing tones and changing notes are to be taken quickly—and in the suspensions, to be introduced preferably in the soprano. Since the latter invariably resolve downward, one must always start again in a higher position (in mm. 3, 9, etc.).

74. From the first of the 12 *Sonate da camera,* Op. 4

¹ Upper part in mm. 9 and 10:

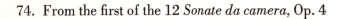

CHAPTER 5
Thoroughbass in the 18th Century

Features of the Thoroughbass Teachings of Mattheson, Heinichen, C. P. E. Bach, and Quantz

In the Baroque era, the years 1700–50 signify the phase of the High Baroque, with its culmination in the works of Bach and Handel. At the same time these are the years of the undisputed domination of the thoroughbass, which is now indispensable in any kind of music except pieces of a contrapuntal nature for only one instrument. Even the two-part keyboard pieces of this period require filling-in with inner voices (see the comments that precede No. 110). It is only natural that the great thoroughbass methods should have arisen at this time, but they are now no longer especially intended as instructors in practical performance, as in the 17th century, but rather as fundamental, methodical harmony treatises. They frequently present first a detailed introduction to music in general, then a systematic theory of harmony, and occasionally a specific method of composition, together with numerous digressions through every conceivable area of music, and they entertain their readers by their air of intimacy and their minuteness of detail.

Among the thoroughbass methods with which I am familiar, the most valuable practice material is contained in Mattheson's *Grand Method of Thoroughbass (Grosse Generalbass-Schule) consisting of three divisions, namely: a preparation in fundamentals; 24 easy exercises; then 24 difficult examples; arranged in such a manner that he who grasps the first part well, and applies it correctly to the other two parts, knows well then how to use what is contained therein, and may be called a master of thoroughbass playing* (Hamburg, 1731).

In the following examples, the aim should be not only to realize the *basso continuo* correctly, but to find good, flowing, cantabile upper parts. The texture need not be four-part, but can be broken up into figuration; Mattheson gives advice about that in the explanations joined to each example. "It is not enough that one plays nonchalantly along, in a routine manner; rather one must know at the same time that he is master of the keyboard and has some judgment about those matters which, be it noted, are obviously not written for poor beginners. . . . Rather, it is assumed that whoever puts his hand to this will have already grasped the beginning fundamentals from good books, but mostly by his own achievement."

Johann Mattheson: Five Examples from his *Grosse Generalbass-Schule* (1731)

75. Example 21 of the Third Part

"At the beginning, thirds should be played note-for-note . . . and the bass should go along in octaves . . . in measures 3 through 6, take octave leaps in the upper part . . . do the same when the figure occurs again in the bass."

Similarly in measures 9ff:

Measure 17:

Measures 27 and 28:

Measures 31 and 32:

76. Example 14 of the Second Part

"I frankly admit that I have not yet seen any piece in this key, but I shall prove to anyone who wishes it that there is no chord in it which one does not come across every day, and often, in other pieces."

77. Example 22 of the Second Part

"In measures 11 through 14, the right hand can play the same thing that the bass has in the next four measures. I don't say that this must be done, but only that it would sound very well, and at the same time the conduct of the parts seems to call for it."

"Measures 26 through 28 are best brought out with full chords, thus:"

"In measures 48 through 55, it would not sound badly to play the right hand as shown in the following manner. In so doing one should not forget that the harmony in the bass must be as full as possible, although it has not been possible to show this here in the notes."

[Measures 60–68:] "I shall write out a few measures here for the student as I, in my humble opinion, believe they ought to be played and varied. Let him who is clever enough to improve upon them do so by all means."

78. Example 5 of the Second Part

"In moving from measures 5–6, 7–8, 15–16, 41–43, and 47–49, since the bass remains stationary, the right hand can descend an octave conjunctly . . . e.g., in measures 5–6:"

"Measures 34ff. may be embellished in many different ways; we wish to show here only the easiest of them . . ."

"From measure 41 on, it would be suitable (in case one plays alone) to invent something cantabile and elegant with the right hand, like an actual melody."

79. Example 2 of the Third Part

"This exercise can be played in the manner of a toccata, or at least like a pleasing toccatina, and the two eighth notes in the first measure, each followed by an eighth rest, indicate that the upper part may repeat what the bass has just played."

Measure 6:

"In measure 13, the chords are broken up most appropriately, in a convenient or deliberate manner, into sixteenth notes."

"This same manner of breaking up chords is very easy, and makes an effect that sounds 'right'."

Measures 24–27:

From the thoroughbass method of Heinichen, Chapter 6: "Concerning ornamented thoroughbass":

"The art of ornamented thoroughbass consists of this: that one does not always play the chords in an ordinary manner, but introduces here and there an embellishment in all the parts (especially in the top voice in the right hand, which stands out very prominently). One thereby gives more grace to the accompaniment, which is ordinarily performed very perfunctorily in a four-part and—upon occasion—five- and six-part accompaniment."

80.

"Instead of this poor kind of accompaniment, it would come off much more elegantly thus:"

"The following example would be very plainly accompanied in this manner."

81.

"Now to remedy this, and to give it a better turn, especially in the upper voice, one can . . . either 1) divide the accompaniment between both hands . . . or 2) undertake the full-voiced accompaniment with the left hand alone and thereby enable the right hand with more ease to invent a separate song or melody to the bass, as far as our ideas, taste, and talent will allow."

For 1):

Upper voice for 2):

From Carl Philipp Emanuel Bach's *Versuch über die wahre Art das Klavier zu spielen* ("Essay on the true manner of playing keyboard instruments") : "Part II, in which the principles of accompaniment and improvisation are treated." Berlin, 1762:

"The most distinctive part of this book, that which makes it different from all books on thoroughbass known until now, concerns elegant accompaniment."

From the introduction: "The organ, harpsichord, piano, and clavichord are the keyboard instruments most commonly used for accompaniment. . . . The organ is indispensable in church music, because of its fugues, big choruses, and generally legato character. The organ promotes splendor and preserves order. But when recitatives and arias occur in church music, a harpsichord must be used, especially when the inner voices of a single accompaniment allow the singer complete freedom to embellish. Unfortunately, one hears only too often how barren the performance sounds without the accompaniment of a harpsichord. This latter instrument, moreover, is indispensable in opera and in chamber performances because of such arias and recitatives.

"The piano and the clavichord are best in supporting a performance in which the greatest refinements of taste are found . . .

"Therefore, no piece can be well executed without the accompaniment of a keyboard instrument. Even in the loudest music, in operas—even in outdoor music, where one would certainly think it impossible to hear the slightest sound of the cembalo—one misses it if it is not there. If one listens to it from an elevated position one can hear every note clearly. I speak from experience, and anyone can prove this for himself.

". . . The most perfect accompaniment for a soloist is a keyboard instrument together with a cello, and no one can deny this . . .

". . . We are no longer content with an accompaniment in which someone plays as a real musical pedant would—that is, nothing more than what the figures indicate . . . we demand something more.

"This 'something more' has been the occasion for continuing my *Essay*, and may be said to be the most particular object of my teaching. I shall attempt to develop accompanists who will follow the rules most accurately but with good taste at the same time.

"Accompaniment can be in one, two, three, four, or more voices. Accompaniment in four and more voices throughout is suitable for large ensembles, for music worked out in contrapuntal style such as fugues, and in general for pieces which do not demand much exercise of taste . . .

"Accompaniment in three or fewer voices is used only for delicate effects, when the taste, performance, or mood of a piece calls for discretion in the harmony. . . ."

(C. P. E. Bach then gives—in the chapters on appoggiaturas, passing tones, and dotted appoggiaturas—very detailed instructions about the treatment of non-harmonic tones in the accompaniment.)

From Chapter 29, "Concerning Performance": ". . . The fewer parts in which a piece is set, the more elegant must the accompaniment be. A solo, or a solo aria, therefore, offers the best opportunity for judging an accompanist . . .

"The beauty of a good accompaniment does not consist in many loud and gaudy passages that are devised without any kind of order . . . The accompanist can best distinguish himself . . . if he allows a simple steadiness and a noble simplicity to be felt in his accompaniment, and on that account does not disturb the brilliant performance of the soloist . . .

"Among the various features of performance, we may begin by considering loudness and softness, and we find that of all instruments . . . the one-manual harpsichord embarrasses the accompanist most because of this very matter of *forte* and *piano*. There is nothing else for him to do than to try to correct this imperfection of the instrument by an increase or decrease in the number of voices in the harmony.

"Consequently . . . because of the various ways in which their loudness and softness may be gradually changed, the clavichord and the pianoforte have many advantages over the harpsichord and organ . . .

"The rules that can be given in general about loud and soft on an organ and on a harpsichord with two keyboards are as follows: *Fortissimo* and *forte* are taken on the louder manual. On it, all the notes of the consonant chords can be played with the left hand, as well as the consonant notes of the dissonant chords when the realization of the bass permits it. . . . The mere doubling of the bass with the octave in the left hand likewise has a penetrating effect, and is therefore indispensable, provided that these notes are not very fast and can be easily executed. . . . If, though . . . passagework occurs that can not be well brought off by one hand in octaves, one can double the principal notes, at least, and play the others without doubling them:

82.

"In *mezzo forte*, the left hand can play only the bass note on the louder manual, while the right hand plays the rest of the chord on the softer manual. Where *piano* is required, both hands play on the softer manual.

Pianissimo is produced also on this manual through the use of fewer voices in the chords . . .

"The first note after a fermata or general pause is preferably taken loudly. . . . If the soloist has a long-held note—which, according to the canons of good performance, begins with a *pianissimo*, gradually swells to a *fortissimo*, and is reduced gradually to a *pianissimo* again—the accompanist should follow it accordingly, and very precisely . . .

"The notes present in a given chord which can be kept in the chord immediately following it should be held. In this way . . . the accompaniment is given a cantabile effect . . .

"The execution of sixteenth notes in the following examples sounds very dull in an Adagio if there is no dot between them. One would do well in performance, therefore, to make up for the absence of the dot.

83.

[hence performed thus:

"If several parts have to be played pizzicato at the same time as the bass, the accompanist should cease playing and leave the performance of these to the cello and double bass . . .

"In slow or moderate tempos, points of rest are generally held longer than they are written, especially if the bass has the same notes and rests . . . as the other voices. . . . Through this way of playing, the musical idea is given an emphasis that causes it to stand out . . .

"In cadential trills, there is most often a retard, regardless of the tempo, though not, however, if bass notes continue during the trill:

84.

"As objectionable as an accompaniment is in which the upper part continually doubles the melody of the principal voice, at times it is necessary —and consequently permitted—at the beginning of a rapid piece, especially when the latter is for two parts. In that case it is played together in both hands, because of the tempo . . .

"If the right hand goes too low in register as the result of many downward-resolving dissonances, one must seize every . . . opportunity, especially during long-held bass notes, and in consonant chords . . . to return gradually and in a proper manner to the higher register . . .

From Chapter 32: "Concerning Certain Refinements of Accompaniment." "Among the refinements of accompaniment belong especially progressions in thirds with the bass. . . . Three-voiced and, in most cases, two-voiced accompaniments . . . are preferable . . .

85.

At times, in these progressions, the thirds are mingled with sixths . . .

86.

[Notated:]   [Performed:]

"An elegant kind of accompaniment, which is not always confined to the same number of inner voices, occasionally allows certain skips through the chord in the right hand, [especially in] . . . musical ideas which permit: a) imitation, b) sustained notes, c) passage work . . .

87.

a)

b)

c)

"The divided accompaniment [i.e. the use of open position] is an important refinement that occurs very often . . .

88.

"The necessary filling out of long notes also belongs to the refinements of accompaniment . . .

89.   [Execution:]

[Execution:]

From Chapter 33: "About Imitation": "Imitations come under those ideas which are customarily altered upon repetition. An accompanist must share in this varying . . ."

90.

From J. J. Quantz: *Versuch einer Anweisung die Flöte traversiere zu spielen* ("Essay at a Method of Playing the Transverse Flute"), Chapter XI: "About Good Performance in Singing and Playing in General":

"Musical performance may be compared with the delivery of an orator. An orator and a musician have . . . basically the same goal, namely to conquer the hearts of men, to arouse or subdue their passions, and to transport the listener now into this emotion, now into that.

"A good performance must first of all be clear and intelligible . . . furthermore, full and rounded . . . also, light and flowing . . . and finally, expressive and appropriate for every passion that arises.

"*About the manner of playing Allegro:* The simple song must be embellished and made pleasing by means of appoggiaturas and other little essential ornaments, in accordance with the emotion that evokes them each time. That which is splendid tolerates little in the way of such addition, but whatever is brought to it must be loftily executed. The flattering demands appoggiaturas, slurred notes, and a tender expression. The gay, on the other hand, demands neatly finished trills, mordents, and a jesting performance. Allegro does not allow for much in the way of arbitrary variation . . . but if it is desirable to vary anything, this should be done only at the repetition. One should not embellish beautiful song-like themes . . . and brilliant passage work, but only themes that do not make a strong impression.

"*About the manner of playing Adagio:* We can play Adagio pieces . . . either in the French or the Italian manner. The first way demands . . . appoggiaturas, whole- and half-trills [the half-trill is the inverted mordent. Ed.], mordents . . . and the like, but otherwise no extensive passage work nor any great addition of arbitrary ornamentation:

91.

"In playing Adagio in the Italian manner, in addition to these little French ornaments, we try to bring to it artistic embellishments that are extended, but that are in agreement with the harmony:

92.

"Alternating *piano* and *forte* . . . is that musical light-and-shade (*chiaroscuro*) that must be expressed here by the player, and which is of the utmost necessity.

"*About keyboard performance in particular:* Not all those who understand thoroughbass are for that reason alone good accompanists. One person must learn through rules, another from experience and, in the last analysis, from his own musical feeling. The general rule is that one should always play in four parts, but in good accompaniment it is often preferable not to adhere to this rule too rigidly . . . and so an accompanist must act more according to the particular situation rather than according to the general rules of thoroughbass.

"Consonances give complete rest and contentment to the soul; dissonances, on the other hand, arouse disturbance in it. In playing, the more a dissonance stands out from all the other notes . . . the more impact it makes on the ear. But the more vexing the thing that disturbs our pleasure, the more agreeable is the pleasure that follows thereafter. It is just this excitation of the various passions that is also the reason why dissonances in general must be attacked more vigorously than consonances.

". . . On a harpsichord with two keyboards, one has the advantage of having *pianissimo* at his disposal on the upper manual. On a pianoforte, however, whatever is called for can be brought about in the most convenient way, for, more than any other keyboard instrument, this one has within itself the necessary resources for good accompaniment.

". . . Imitations that consist of running or melodious passages make a better effect when they are doubled an octave higher in the right hand than if one accompanies them in a full-voiced texture. One can proceed in a similar manner with imitation at the unison.

"When the bass leaves its usual register and has something to play in the tenor register—which it is accustomed to do more often in vocal music —the right hand must accompany with few voices, and quite close to the left hand; in that way what follows afterwards in the bass register may be expressed so much the more effectively.

"*About Recitative:* There are certain recitatives in which the bass and the other instruments for which they are scored have a definite subject or a rhythmical movement in notes that continue to sound, regardless of the rests in the solo voice. These must be performed in a strictly rhythmical manner, in order to keep together well. The other kinds of recitative are, according to their nature, sung sometimes slowly, sometimes quickly, regardless of the measure, even though they are divided into measures in the notation. The change to a new harmony must take place very quickly, immediately upon the ending of the previous chord. In rapid declamation, the accompanist must refrain from arpeggiating, all the more so if the harmony changes frequently. Recitatives accompanied by instruments capable of producing sustained tones tolerate arpeggios particularly well. In accompanying recitative, no other ornaments and graces are used on keyboard instruments."

Nine Movements for a Solo Instrument with *Basso Continuo*
by Corelli, Handel, and Bach

93. Arcangelo Corelli: Gavotte from Violin Sonata No. 10

94. Arcangelo Corelli: Giga from the same Sonata

G. F. Handel: Three Pieces from *15 Solos for a German Flute, Hoboy,
or Violin, with a Thoroughbass for the Harpsichord, or Bass Violin,
opera prima* (1724)

95. Adagio from Sonata No. 5

96. Bourrée from the same Sonata

97. Allegro from Sonata No. 3

J. S. Bach: Movements from *Sonata II for flute and Continuo* and the *Musical Offering*

98. Menuetto I from the Sonata in C Major for Flute and Continuo

The harpsichord part of this Minuet is the only accompaniment of a thoroughbass sonata realized by Bach himself.

99. Menuetto II[1]

Menuetto I Da Capo

100. Trio Movement from the *Musical Offering* (1747); Thoroughbass Realization by J. P. Kirnberger (1721–83)[2]

---

[1] While not indicated by Keller, Menuetto II is the "Trio" of No. 98. As in the latter, the treble part is performed by the flute, and the continuo part should proceed in a manner in keeping with that of No. 98. [Ed.]

[2] Compare with the realization by Max Seiffert (Publications of the *Neue Bachgesellschaft*, XXIX, 2) [H. K.]

Next to the pedantically correct realization of Kirnberger we give an example of one made in a freer manner by J. S. Bach himself, perhaps one of the most beautiful ever written: the third movement of the B-minor *Sonata a Cembalo obbligato e Flauto traverso*, in which the harpsichord is not thematically equal with the flute, as in the other movements, but accompanies it in a way that one can imagine Bach himself improvised.

101.

³ The student should try to complete the second part of the movement himself. [H. K.]

CHAPTER 6

Thoroughbass in the Sacred Music of the 18th Century

The task that faces the keyboard player most frequently, and one to which every conductor will give careful attention, is the realization of the thoroughbass in Bach's cantatas and Passions. The remarks of Max Seiffert in the Bach *Jahrbuch* of 1904 were fundamental for the present cultivation of Bach's music. In them he called for the following: The revival of the historical instruments, the proper relationship in strength between the winds and the strings and between the orchestra and the chorus, the proper disposition of forces, proper dynamics, phrasing, and realization of the *basso continuo*. Concerning the last item, Seiffert said that the organ and harpsichord should complement one another, and that the organ belongs with the chorus: "The organ joins in when the chorus enters, and stops when it does; it accomodates the changes of its harmony to the movement of the chorus. In doing that, it ties together wherever possible what the chorus breaks up into rhythmically lively motifs; 'it promotes splendor and preserves order.' [Quotation from C. P. E. Bach; see p. 49.] The harpsichord, on the other hand, is suited primarily to the orchestra. . . . The organ is therefore silent in the instrumental introductions and interludes, for it is here that the harpsichord speaks. On the other hand, the harpsichord ceases its activity as soon as the choral voices sing in stretches without accompaniment. . . . In all cases where chorus and orchestra unite, organ and harpsichord also play in concert."

In the opinion of the editor, everyone should be advised to follow this rule in day-to-day usage; it ought not, though, be followed as though it were a rigid system, as often happens today. A conductor or arranger, if he wants to have unusual effects, will use the organ and harpsichord in different ways. Artistic feeling must take precedence over mere historical correctness (which is taken for granted, of course). The arrangements by Eusebius Mandyczewski of Bach's arias and duets in the publications of the *Neue Bachgesellschaft* may be cited as exemplary models of realization; as models of the opposite kind there might be noted many of the older piano-vocal scores of Breitkopf and Härtel, with their thick and often unmusical settings. Lack of space forbids considering all the editions in this connection, but I have shown for comparison, on pages 75–76, the beginning of the alto aria of Cantata 106 in seven different versions. The assiduous student of thoroughbass is strongly advised to scrutinize very critically any printed editions or manuscripts of continuo parts that come to hand, and to compare them with the original score. The principal aim of the present method is to carry him far enough so that he will prefer to accompany from the figured bass part itself (which means, nowadays, from the full score).

102. J. S. Bach: Chorale from Cantata 140, *Wachet auf, ruft uns die Stimme* ("Awake, the Voice is Calling Us")

Zion hears the watchman sing,
For joy her heart doth leap,
She watches and rises hastily.
Her Friend comes down from heaven in splendor,
Strong in grace, mighty in truth,
Her light becomes bright, her star arises.
Come now, Thou worthy paragon,
Lord Jesus, Son of God, Hosanna!
We follow to the hall of joy
And share the Supper of the Lord.

This piece was included by Bach in the *Sechs Choräle*, the so-called *Schübler Chorales*, as an organ trio without figures.

Anyone who has difficulty in reading old clefs should first go all through each part alone, but in a steady tempo.

103. J. S. Bach: Recitative and Arioso from Cantata 60, *O Ewigkeit, du Donnerwort* ("O Eternity, Thou Word of Thunder")

¹ Or on two manuals of an organ with contrasting registration. [H. K.]

zu ver-schlin-gen droht; viel - leicht ist sie be-reits ver-flucht zu e - wi-gem Ver - der - ben.

(Arioso)

Se - - lig sind die To - ten, se - - lig sind die To - ten, die To-ten, die in

(Rec.)

dem Her - ren ster - ben.   Wenn ich im Her - ren ster - be, ist dann die Se - lig-keit mein Teil und

Er - be? Der Leib wird ja der Wür-mer Spei - se! Ja, wer-den mei - ne Glie - der zu Staub und Er - de

wie - der, da ich ein Kind des To-des hei - ße, so schein ich ja im Gra - be zu ver - der - ben.

(Arioso)

Se - - lig sind die To-ten, se - - lig sind die To-ten, die To-ten, die in ___ dem Herren

ster - ben, die in dem Her-ren ster-ben, von nun ___ an, von nun an, von nun ___ an, von nun an, se -

- - lig sind die To-ten, die To-ten, die in ___ dem Her-ren ster - - - ben, von nun an.

(Rec.)

Wohl-an! soll ich von nun an se-lig sein: so stel-le dich, o Hoff-nung, wie-der ein. Mein Leib kann oh - ne

Furcht im Schla - fe ruhn, der Geist kann ei - nen Blick in je - ne Freu - de tun.

Dialogue (between Fear and the Voice of the Holy Ghost, based on the
Revelation of St. John, 14, 13)

Recitative:
Death continues to be hated by mortal nature, and it almost drags hope down to
the ground.

Arioso
Blessed are the dead . . .

(Rec.)
Ah! What great danger the soul imagines when entering on the road to death!
Perhaps death—the jaws of hell—frightens it as if threatening to devour it; per-
haps it is already cursed with eternal destruction.

(Arioso)
Blessed are the dead who die in the Lord.

(Rec.)
If I die in the Lord, is blessedness my share and my inheritance? The body becomes the food of worms! Yes, my members become dust and earth again, since I
am called a child of death, and so I seem doomed, indeed, to the grave.

(Arioso)
Blessed are the dead . . . who die in the Lord . . .
Henceforth, blessed are the dead who die in the Lord . . .

(Rec.)
Now then! If I am henceforth to be blessed, appear to me again, O hope! My
body then can rest in sleep without fear, my spirit can catch a glimpse of that joy.

104. J. S. Bach: Aria from Cantata 61, *Nun komm', der Heiden Heiland*
("Come Now, Thou Saviour of the Gentiles")

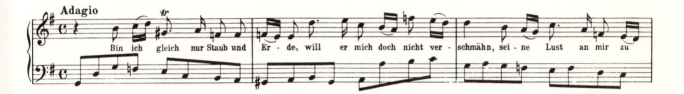

Open thyself, my heart entire . . .
Jesus comes and enters in . . .

Adagio:

Although I am like dust and earth,
He will not disdain me;
His pleasure in gazing upon me will be
To see that I have become His dwelling place.
O, how blessed . . . shall I be . . .

Suggestions for performance:

105. J. S. Bach: Aria for Alto from Cantata 106, *Gottes Zeit is die aller-beste Zeit* ("God's Time is the Best Time of All")

In Thy hands . . . I commend my spirit . . .
Thou hast redeemed me, Lord, Thou true God . . .

For comparison, the first two measures of the aria in seven different realizations follow (the bass being as it is in the original):

1) Breitkopf & Härtel, piano-vocal score:

2) Robert Franz (piano-vocal score published by F. Leuckart):

3) *Neue Bachgesellschaft* (O. Schröder):

4) Peters Edition (G. Rösler):

5) Arthur Willner (Philharmonia Pocket Scores):

6) Max Seiffert (Breitkopf & Härtel):

7) Suggestion by the editor:

106. Francesco Gasparini: Motet for four voices and bass, *Adoramus Te*[2]

[2] Generally held to have been a work of W. A. Mozart, according to recent investigations this piece is actually by Gasparini. [H. K.] (The composition is printed in the Complete Edition of Mozart's Works, Series 3, No. 30, p. 121, 1880; Ed.)

We adore Thee, O Christ, and we bless Thee,
For through Thy holy cross . . . Thou hast redeemed the world . . .

CHAPTER 7
Thoroughbass in Two-Part Keyboard Music: Unfigured Basses

G. P. Telemann: Three Minuets (from *Sept fois sept et un Menuet*), 1728

If the melody is played by a violin or flute, the realizations of the bass should be similar to those in Nos. 93–100. If, however, the minuets are played as keyboard pieces, only as many inner parts should be played as are necessary and convenient:

107.

108.

109.

Telemann's minuets with figured bases may serve as preparatory studies for that part of thoroughbass playing which, while not the most important, is perhaps the most attractive—the performance of unfigured music of the first half of the 18th century that is notated in two parts; pieces that sound dry and thin without such filling-out (the latter must be discreet but imaginative). Of course, this procedure should not be extended to include pieces of a contrapuntal nature such as Bach's Two-part Inventions, but it would include the minuets and other small pieces in the *style galant* such as those in the *Notenbüchlein* of Anna Magdalena Bach, the new Schott edition of Handel's keyboard music, and others. In this connection, attention should be called to the Fantasies of Telemann (new edition by Max Seiffert, Berlin, 1923), which have been little known until now, but which belong among the best works of this genre.

G. P. Telemann: *Fantasies pour le clavessin; 3 Douzaines* (after 1737)

110. From the First Fantasy of the Second Dozen

111. The Ninth Fantasy of the Second Dozen

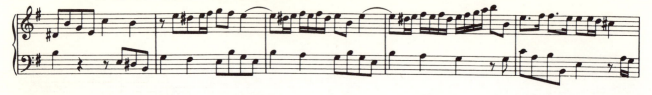

Flateusement D.C.

112. The Third Fantasy of the First Dozen

Vivace D.C.

In the Foreword to Volume 32 (the Chamber Duets) of the Complete Edition of Handel's works, Chrysander writes: "Whether with or without cello, the modifications of the accompaniment that can take place here are almost endless. None of those who have assisted with keyboard realizations in the Handelgesellschaft Edition has been able or willing to supply anything other than one of the various possible ways of harmonizing this music. The only immutable and constant factors here are the fixed, basic rules of basso continuo. And since each one, for this reason, has complete freedom to arrange the harmony, the editors of the present edition also claim the same freedom for their accompaniments printed here." The keyboard accompaniments to the last six duets, which are from Handel's most mature period, are by Johannes Brahms (Peters Edition).

113. G. F. Handel: Chamber Duet for Soprano, Alto, and Thoroughbass, *Fronda leggier' e mobile* (1743)

Fron-da leg-gier' e mo - - - bi-le, fia - to d'au-rett' i - sta - bi-le, fia - to d'au-rett' i - sta - bi-le è

Fron-da leggier' e mo - bi-le, fron-da leggier' e

sempr' il tuo fa-vor, sort' in-co-stan - - - te! Fronda leggier' e mo -

mo - - - - bi-le, fia-to d'au-rett' i - sta - bi-le, fia-to d'au-rett' i - sta-bi-le,

- - - bi-le, fronda leggier' e mo - bi-le, fia-to d'au-rett' i - sta - bi-le, fia-to d'au-rett' i -

fia - to d'au-rett' i - sta - bi-le è sempr' il tuo fa - vor, è sempr' il tuo fa-vor, è sempr' il tuo fa-vor

sta - bi-le, fia-to d'au-rett' i - sta - bi-le è sempr' il tuo fa - vor, è sempr' il tuo fa-vor sort' in-co-

sort' in-co-stan - - - te, sort' in-co-stan - - -

stan - - - te, sort' in-co-stan -

Andante Larghetto

Allegro:
  The light and fickle leaf,
  The changeable breath of the zephyr,
  Such is always thy favor, o inconstant fate! . . .

Andante Larghetto:
  Wise the heart that is free, and puts no faith
  In the deceptive smile of thy countenance . . .

Summary

The player who wishes to turn to account what he has learned in this method, whether as accompanist, director, or arranger and editor of older music, will try to make himself familiar with the performance practice of thoroughbass beyond the narrow limits sketched here. In addition to the literature indicated on pp. *xi–xiii* above, the following may be recommended for this purpose: Robert Haas, *Aufführungspraxis der Musik* ("The Performance Practice of Music"), Athenaion-Verlag, 1931, and the article *Generalbass* ("Thoroughbass") by Fritz Oberdörfer in the encyclopedia *Die Musik in Geschichte und Gegenwart*, where the reader will also find a satisfactory number of references to special studies. For the practical musician, a synopsis of questions concerning thoroughbass may be given here in concise form as a closing section.

Thoroughbass, originally only a technical expedient, quickly became the dominating style principle of the whole period. In it and through it a spasmodic transition was achieved from the epoch of contrapuntal, linear composition to the homophonic style founded on the predominance of harmony, and the bass, as the support of the entire tonal structure, received an importance it never had before or since. With one stroke composition was made easy. Perhaps in no other epoch was so much music composed so quickly— and so superficially—as at that time. But the technique of thoroughbass developed together with the period itself. Thus in the early Baroque the question of technique still remains in the background, but the matter of diversity of sound and its realization comes to the fore. In the late phase of Bach and his contemporaries, thoroughbass became predominantly a question of music theory. In the 19th century it is relegated to the teaching of elementary theory and in general is no longer cultivated in actual practice. Thoroughbass had to withdraw from the scene when (from Rameau on) the transition from thinking in intervals to thinking in terms of harmonic functions was effected; in so doing, the way was made clear for Viennese Classicism.

In the enormous amount and variety of music composed between 1600 and 1750, one is ever and again astonished at how simple the harmony is, how restricted the store of harmony with which composers had to make do, and with which they did make do, namely the triads on each degree of the scale with their inversions and their respective seventh chords. The latter play an important part from Corelli on (see Nos. 73 and 94). In the thoroughbass period there is not as great a harmonic difference among individual composers as in the 19th century; rather, harmony gives the fundamental coloring to the epoch, so to speak.

Thus harmony is the persistent, even the retarding, factor in a period whose development proceeded at first impetuously, then in calmer ways. Thoroughbass playing also shared in this change; therefore the player must know that there is no formula for the whole period, no uniform manner according to which basses should be realized. What is valid for Monteverdi is not so for Handel; what is right for Bach cannot necessarily be applied to Schütz.

The Instruments

There is a distinction between sacred and secular music in this regard. In secular music, at the beginning of the period, we see an almost inconceivable variety of instruments, but this is soon lost. In the church, the organ, of course, was the thoroughbass instrument throughout the whole period. In church music, the bass line was most often played by a *violone* (i.e. a bass viol), and, in a bigger group, by the bassoon also. Registration indications for organists have come down to us from the early Baroque. Viadana, and Praetorius after him, advise the player that in a full-voiced setting he should use a larger number of parts, but not to draw additional stops, so that the singer may not be covered (see p. 30). Monteverdi, on the other hand, gives registration indications for each movement of his *Magnificat*, beginning with the "Principale solo" (by which a very soft sound is to be understood), then through the "Principale, Ottava, e Quintadecima" (i.e. 8' + 4' + 2') up to the "Organo pleno" of the final movement.

From later times we have almost no registration indications, but we can learn Bach's views from his design for the rebuilding of his organ at Mülhausen, in which he wanted to have a 16' Fagott, because "it sounds very delicate in the music," and that he wanted to replace the Gemshorn with a Viola de gamba (undoubtedly for the accompaniment of arias), "where it will agree admirably with the present Salicional 4' in the Rückpositiv." Seiffert's opinion (see p. 65), that in Bach's choral performances the organ doubled the choral parts while the cembalo took over the thoroughbass, has been shown by Schering's investigations to be untenable; with few exceptions the organ was the accompanying instrument in Bach's church music also. The direction to accompany arias with the harpsichord is first found in C. P. E. Bach, and this would no doubt represent a better sound for many arias of J. S. Bach also.

In the secular music of the early Baroque, a distinction was made between the *fundamental* instruments that had to strengthen the harmony—the gravicembalo, chitarrone, and a small organ, among others—and the *ornamenting* instruments that had to make the melody "flowery and lovely"—such as the lute, violin, and spinetta, among many others. How all these instruments could perform together without written parts may appear mysterious to us; seemingly the memory of musicians was trained so that each soon had the whole in mind. But these instruments, according to Cavalieri, should not play together at all times, but "change according to the expression of the music." In 1664, Cesti still called for "four keyboard instruments and two theorboes"; Cavalli was content with three harpsichords. Even in the 18th century the principle was adhered to of keeping the continuo instruments in a fixed numerical proportion to the instruments of the orchestra; Quantz, for example, wanted one harpsichord for every six orchestral violins. Our current practice of performing a Handel oratorio with 200 singers, an orchestra of from 50 to 60 players, and a single cembalo would have found little sanction in the 18th century. Today, however, there is an attempt, and a successful one, to come closer to the old tonal proportions; in the Handel festival performances at Halle the thoroughbass part was very richly represented. This process, however, should not be extended to the recitatives, which should always be accompanied by a single player, so that he can adapt himself to the singer.

In domestic music-making and in chamber music, the lute was occasionally used, also the clavichord; since in most cases this resulted in too weak a tone, accompaniment was entrusted to the harpsichord as a rule. A small one-manual instrument sufficed. The bass line was doubled by the cello, or, if a softer tone was preferred, by the viola da gamba, the player reading from the harpsichordist's score. As a matter of interest it might be noted that in later life C. P. E. Bach and Quantz preferred the new piano, because of its capability of producing nuances, to the inflexible sound of the harpsichord.

A special case arose when the harpsichord was treated in an obbligato or concertizing manner. How was the filling-in accompaniment to be executed? Of J. S. Bach's seven concertos for one harpsichord, that in A major is provided with a second—accompanimental—harpsichord part. In the Concerto in D minor, on the other hand, it is not required anywhere, and it is even less essential to the concertos for two, three, and four harpsichords. In the six Sonatas for Violin and Obbligato Cembalo (likewise in the three Sonatas for Flute and the three for Viola da gamba), the two-part beginnings of the movements (before the right hand of the harpsichordist enters with the theme) are to be performed in thoroughbass style, even where Bach has not written figures. In these purely three-part movements, the tonal balance is shifted considerably in favor of the harpsichord if a stringed instrument doubles the bass. The harpsichord blends tonally with cello or gamba, but the piano does not, so that in a performance in which the piano is used, the doubling stringed bass instrument should not be employed. In this whole question of instruments it should always be kept in mind that at that time there was never any dogmatic idea of one being wrong and another right; rather, it was a question of what was available, and the texture was made richer or thinner according to the place and the occasion. That performances took place even without filling-in, in case of necessity, is shown by titles such as *Violone o* [*or*] *Cimbalo*. Sometimes the organ relinquished a lively passage of figuration to the cello and restricted itself to a simpler bass progression (see p. 74).

The Notation

In his *Exemplarische Organistenprobe* ("Specimen Examination for Organists"), 1719, Mattheson says: "Even though the player works out the bass figuring accurately, there is still a good part—indeed, I might almost say the largest part—left to him and his invention." There was, then, the same freedom in realizing the figuring as there was in the choice of instrument. Frequently figures are lacking, partly because of carelessness, partly because the composer rehearsed the work himself, which was the rule, especially in opera or in circumstances where the player had the full score before him. In larger groups, two copies of the part were used, one for the thoroughbass player, the other for the double bass (or other) performer; Schütz introduced this practice in Germany, Purcell in England.

What should the accompanist make of the figures? In the early period, when figures up to 10, 11, 13, 14 and even beyond were notated, these indicated to the player in what octave-position the obbligato parts moved. Later, when the figures did not go beyond 9, they showed the player the skeleton of the four-part composition he had to realize. In some choral movements of Bach, figures occur that are not contained in the principal voices. It is remarkable that the manner of figuring remained the same throughout the whole epoch; a few efforts at improvement were unsuccessful.

The Techniques of Chord- and Part-Playing

Nowhere do theory and practice lie closer to one another than in thoroughbass. That is why the techniques of chord- and part-playing are mutually involved, one with the other. Normally the left hand plays the bass, the right hand the realization in close position. Viadana, and Praetorius after him, permit playing in open position and with the pedal, at climaxes. It may be recommended that present-day organists use the pedal only in playing a cantus firmus, in pedal points, and at climaxes; otherwise to play with a discreet, fluid 8′ + 4′ registration in the right hand, and an 8′ + 16′ (if the latter is not too thick) in the left. The player would do best to prepare beforehand one registration for the arias, another for the recitatives, and a third for the choral sections, which from then on need be modified only slightly. On the harpsichord, however, the player can achieve dynamic differentiation only through a change from few-voiced to full-voiced playing. For this reason alone it would be meaningless to demand a purity of part-playing that no one would hear, let alone appreciate. The upper part of the accompaniment should not double the melody but remain a third below it, so that no competition with the principal voice is allowed to arise. According to Werckmeister, the accompaniment in general should not be taken above c^2, although Niedt says not over f^2; only Heinichen allows c^3, and that only in exceptional cases. Suspensions should be in the same octave-position in both the accompaniment and the principal part, as far as possible—parallel octaves here would make an unlovely effect. Particularly objectionable is the thoughtlessness of so many modern editions in which a suspension that is dotted in the principal voice: $\begin{smallmatrix}\\4\ 3\end{smallmatrix}$, is put in notes of the same value: $\begin{smallmatrix}\\4\ 3\end{smallmatrix}$ in the realization. C. P. E. Bach even wanted to put dots besides the figures: $\begin{smallmatrix}6.\ \ .5\\4.\ \ .3\end{smallmatrix}$, in order to avoid this. Chords in recitative are to be played short, even on the organ. But if they contain a progression in the upper voice, such as 6 5, it might be better to sustain the whole chord rather than only one voice.

The editions of chamber music of the thoroughbass period that have appeared since that era may be divided into two kinds. In the first belong the arrangements that are often timidly orthodox, being limited mostly to a completely colorless harmonic four-part arrangement in close position. They are unnecessary, for today there are again hundreds of thoroughbass players who can easily improvise such a setting. As Mattheson said: "It is no longer enough today when someone plays nonchalantly along, in a routine manner." The other group is formed by the great virtuosos and practical musicians, who edit sonatas in the way they sound best, without allowing themselves to be disturbed by considerations of music history. This, too, is outmoded today; what we need is artistic freedom on the sound basis of the style principles of the time—more precisely, of the various style phases of the thoroughbass period.

All the pedagogical works impress upon the accompanist that he should never forget that he must not ever encroach upon the soloists; he must think, rather, about how he may accommodate himself to them. The masters of the early Baroque (Viadana, Agazzari, Praetorius), though, affirm and desire that the thoroughbass player should display his art in the interludes, when the singers are silent; that he should undertake embellishments of the vocal part when the singer performs simple notes (see pp. 29–30). Monteverdi even introduces anticipating coloraturas once in the accompaniment of his *Vespro della beata Virgine* ("Pulchra es, anima mea"); Heinichen did not object to adding imitations in the accompaniment—if one could do it!

There are narrow limits in accompaniment, but surely significant musicians have from time to time overstepped them. Kittel, Bach's last pupil, reports thus of his teacher: "When Sebastian Bach performed church music, one of his most capable students always had to accompany at the harpsichord" (presumably this was at the rehearsals). "It may indeed be imagined that no one dared to come forth on such an occasion with some kind of scanty thoroughbass accompaniment. Besides, one had always to be prepared to find Bach's hands and fingers suddenly mingling among the hands and fingers of the player; without further disturbing these, they would supply the accompaniment with volumes of harmonies which impressed the students even more than did the unsuspected presence of their strict teacher." Bach's written instructions and corrections are far removed from such freedom (see Spitta II, 102ff. and 193ff., Eng. transl.), just as is the realization of the first 15 measures of the aria *Empfind ich Höllenangst und Pein* ("I Feel the Terror and Torment of Hell") made by Bach himself:[1]

On the other hand, the harpsichord part of the "Largo e dolce" movement of the Flute Sonata in B minor (see No. 101) can be regarded as an example of a particularly rich original realization. The same is true of the harpsichord part of the first and third movements of the Violin Sonata in E major, as well as others. The ornamented thoroughbass, as Heinichen, Quantz, and C. P. E. Bach teach it (see pp. 49–55) is valid only for their own styles—

---

[1] See the *Zeitschrift für Musikwissenschaft, Jahrg.* 15, *Heft* 5. This is a bass aria from Cantata No. 3, *Ach Gott, wie manches Herzlied* (BGA I, p. 86), and the illustration given here, in Bach's own hand, is described in detail by Helmut Schultz in pp. 225–28 of the issue of the *ZfMW* mentioned above. In the BGA, the instrumental bass is unfigured, and in the MS fragment, Bach's figures break off at the 15th measure. This fragment is transposed down a whole step from the version in BGA; i.e. it is in the *Chorton*, or "church pitch." [Ed.]

that is, for the highly refined, even over-refined, end of the epoch; inferences from them may be applied retroactively to J. S. Bach only with great caution. But in J. S. Bach, too, one should depart from the unvarying use of four-part style, especially in the accompaniment of arias. I have given examples of a free accompaniment which, in spite of its relative independence, remains subordinate to the principal voices, in my realization of two arias with obbligato instruments: *Bereite dich Zion* ("Prepare thyself, Zion") and *Seufzer, Tränen, Kummer, Not* ("Sighs, Tears, Sorrow, Need"), in Bärenreiter Editions, Nos. 2310 and 2311. If the arias in Handel's operas are to be sung with the embellishments that were customary at that time, the accompanist must accommodate himself to this style (see Hellmut Christian Wolff's edition of the Handel opera *Agrippina,* and his remarks there), although such liberties cannot and should not be fixed once and for all: they were improvised by the singer, and the accompanist followed.

Thus the teaching of thoroughbass offers much instruction to the player in need of it, but nowhere does it give inflexible directions; rather, it is content with recommendations, on the basis of which a thoroughbass realization can arise anew each time, according to place, size of group, instrument used, taste, and technique. He who has worked through this method should, as a general rule, no longer use continuo parts that have already been realized, but should play from the score like a true thoroughbass performer, and suit his playing to all the factors just named; he will then have attained the ideal of the accompanist, who reads not his own part but the parts he has to accompany.